INQUIRING ABOUT

COMMUNITIES

HOLT Databank SYSTEM

A SOCIAL SCIENCE PROGRAM

William R. Fielder, General Editor

INQUIRING ABOUT

COMMUNITIES

B. Robert Tabachnick

Professor of Curriculum and Instruction
School of Education
University of Wisconsin

Holt, Rinehart and Winston, Publishers

NEW YORK   TORONTO   LONDON   SYDNEY

Professor William R. Fielder, the General Editor of the HOLT DATABANK SYSTEM, received his Ed.D. in Elementary Education from Stanford University in 1960. Prior to his present position as Professor and Director, Division of Graduate Studies in Education, Oregon State University, he served on the faculties of San Jose State College, Stanford University, Michigan State University, and The Claremont Graduate School and University Center. He has acted as director of a number of educational research projects, including projects in differentiated staffing and instructional television, and has also served as a consultant to local and regional school systems. Professor Fielder is a co-author of *Social Study: Inquiry in Elementary Classrooms* (1966) and a contributor to a variety of professional journals.

Professor B. Robert Tabachnick is the author of this volume in the series, *Inquiring About Communities*. Professor Tabachnick received his Ed.D. in Elementary Curriculum from Stanford University in 1959. He is presently a Professor of Curriculum and Instruction and Educational Policy Studies at the University of Wisconsin at Madison. He is co-author of *Social Study: Inquiry in Elementary Classrooms* (1966), and he has also written articles on the teaching of social studies and children's concept and attitude development.

ACKNOWLEDGMENTS

To Mary Lou Peterson, Supervisor of Local Materials, Madison (Wisc.) Public Schools and Keith Hogle, National Social Studies Consultant for Holt, Rinehart and Winston, who contributed much invaluable material and furnished many stimulating suggestions. Their assistance is deeply appreciated.

For photo research: Lynn Landy and Jane Bouregy
COVER DESIGN: Rita Leydon

Credits for art and text photographs appear on the opposite page.

Art Credits

Credits for drawn art are as follows in alphabetical order:

Angela Adams—2.
Richard Amundsen—13, 16–17, 69, 72–73, 94–95, 97–99.
Gerry Contreras—48, 54, 57, 106, 109.
Arthur Cummings—40–43.
Allen Davis—20 *bottom*.
Hugh Frost—121 *top*.
Bill George—39.
Ethel Gold—10–12, 15, 35–38.
Robert Goldstein—107.
Meryl Henderson—4–5.
Fred Irvin—74.
Tad Krumeich—8–9, 24, 80–81, 121 *bottom*.

Dora Leder—21, 151.
Mary Michal—85, 124–125.
Eleanor Mill—44–45, 67, 142–143, 146–147.
Raoul Mina Mora—26 *bottom*, 58–61, 65–66, 82–83, 87–91, 104, 122.
Herb Mott—113, 116, 120, 138–141.
Larry Noble—29, 108.
Ruth Sanderson—150.
Joanne Scribner—18–19, 126–127.
Bob Shein—50–53, 55–56.
Philip Smith—3.
Kyuzo Tsugami—26 *top*, 31, 49, 92.

Photo Credits

Brown—Brown Brothers; Culver—Culver Pictures; EP—Editorial Photocolor; Magnum—Magnum Photos; NAS—National Audubon Society; PR—Photo Researchers; Rapho—Rapho-Guillumette.

UNIT 1   6—*top* N. Simon; *bottom* Norman Lightfoot/*both* PR. **7**—*both* Tom McHugh/PR. **14**—*top* Grant Heilman; *bottom* Bruce Roberts/Rapho. **20**—*top* Ian Berry/Magnum. **22**—W. B. Finch/EP. **23**—EP. **25**—Jeanne Tabachnick. **27**—Grant Heilman. **28**—H. R. & W. Photo by Richard H. Goff, Jr. **30**—*both* Brown. **32**—Brown.
UNIT 2   34—*top* Donald S. Heintzelman/NAS; *bottom* William Jahoda/NAS. **46**—*top* Grant Heilman; *bottom* H. R. & W. Photo by Darwin Chen. **47**—*top* George Holton; *bottom* Russ Kinne/*both* PR. **50**—Eric Lessing/Magnum. **52**—H. R. & W. Photo by Russell Dian. **54**—*top* Wayne Miller/Magnum; *bottom* H. R. & W. Photo by Richard Weiss. **56**—H. R. & W. Photo by Russell Dian. **62**—Courtesy of Mt. Wilson and Palomar Observatories.
UNIT 3   64—Brown. **68**—*top* H. R. & W. Photo by Owen Franken, Stock, Boston; *bottom* EP. **70–71**—EP. **75**—Laurence Lowry/Rapho. **76**—*top left* H. R. & W. Photo by Charles Biasiny; *top right* Artur Tress; *bottom* Burt Glinn/Magnum. **78**—*top* Inge Morath/Magnum; *bottom* Artur Tress. **79**—*top* Artur Tress; *bottom* Charles Harbutt/Magnum. **86**—*top* Mauro E. Mujica/EP; *bottom* Van Bucher/PR.
UNIT 4   100—*top left* The Granger Collection; *top right* Rhode Island Historical Society; *bottom* Paul Fusco/Magnum. **102**—The Pierpont Morgan Library. **103**—*top* Culver; *bottom* Joe Munroe/PR. **105**—Charles Harbutt/Magnum. **110**—Jeanne Tabachnick. **111**—*top* Van Bucher/PR; *bottom* Jeanne Tabachnick. **112; 114–115; 117–119**—Jeanne Tabachnick.
UNIT 5   128—*top* Culver; *bottom* National Aeronautics and Space. **129**—*top* Culver; *bottom* H. R. & W. Photo by Charles Biasiny. **130–131**—Brown. **132–133**—Culver. **134**—Brown. **135**—*top* Library of Congress; *bottom* Brown. **136**—*top* H. R. & W. Photo; *bottom* © Zimmerman/FPG. **137**—*top* H. R. & W. Photo; *bottom left* H. R. & W. Photo by Charles Biasiny; *bottom right* Roy Stevens/Courtesy of the Ford Foundation. **144–145**—H. R. & W. Photo. **148**—*both* Culver. **149**—Courtesy of the General Motors Corporation. **152**—H. R. & W. Photo by Russell Dian.

Contents

1

Being a Person

What is a person?
Do you think you know?

Here are people doing things.
What do you think the people are
doing?
There are some animals, too.
What do you think the animals are
doing?

Look at all these...!
How are they different from one
another?
Think of one word you could use for
all of them.

In some ways bears act like people. If you saw some bears in your classroom would you think they were people coming to visit you?

Bears can be as different from one
another as people are different from
other people.
The next page is for bears only.

8

Oops!
Something is wrong with this page
for bears only.
What is wrong?

Did you find two people with all
those bears?
People look like other people.
Look carefully at the people in these
pictures.
How does each person look like
every other person?

Look at the bears you saw before.
How does a bear look different from
a person?

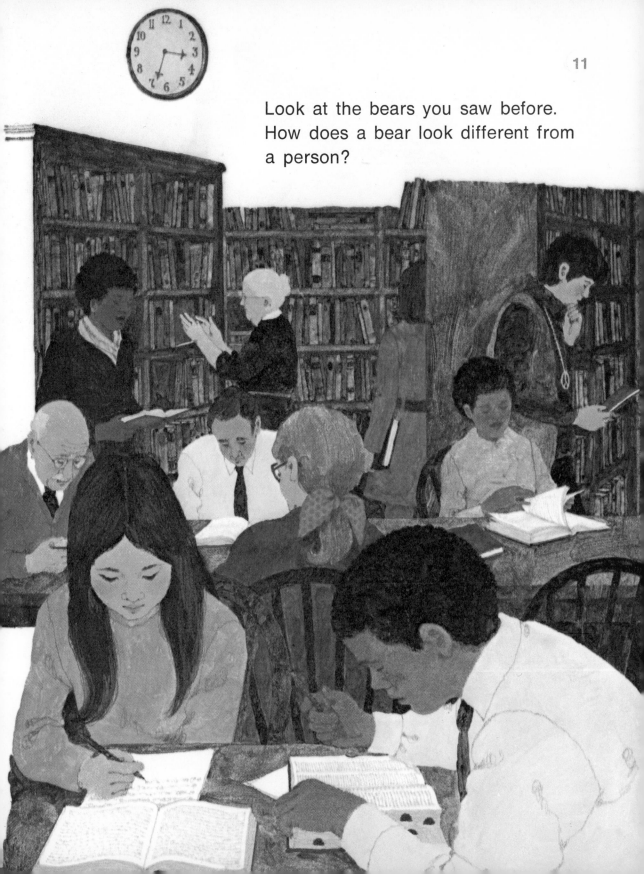

People look like people.
People also act like people.
Another word for person is human.
What are some human ways to act?
What is the human thing to do?

Some of these bees are doing a wiggle
waggle sort of dance.
The dance will tell worker bees where
they can find nectar.

The nectar is sweet stuff deep inside
flowers.
Bees use nectar to make honey.

When you want to tell someone to
go and get some food you do not
do a wiggle waggle dance.
You say some words in sentences.
You use language.

One beaver in the water hears
something that scares him.
He smacks the water with his tail
and warns the other beavers.

People use language to warn about
danger coming.
When too much rain falls into a river
the river may run over and flood the
land.
People must leave their homes and
go to a safe dry place on high land.

A tornado is a fast whirling wind that
can blow a house down.
The TV announcer is warning that
a tornado is coming.
She does not smack her tail.
She uses language.

When a tornado is near, people stay
inside their homes.
They go down into a cellar.
They listen to their radio till they
hear someone say the tornado has
gone away.

People use language.
You are using language right now.
Using language is a human thing to do.

Most people live near other people.
That is a human thing to do.
People live together in groups.
Some of the groups are small.

Some people live near many many other people.

A small group lives in each house.
The small group is a family.
These families live near other
families in a community.
A community has a large group of
families living together.

Many families live in each one of
these buildings.
The families in these buildings
are a large group.
They are a community.

With the help of tools people can do
things they could not do by
themselves.

When there is work to do people use tools to help them do it.
Using tools is a human thing to do.
Tools can make you stronger.

Tools can make you taller.

Tools can make you smaller.

What tools help you see people who
are far away?

People are very good at dreaming.
It is a human thing to do.
People think about things that
happened long ago.

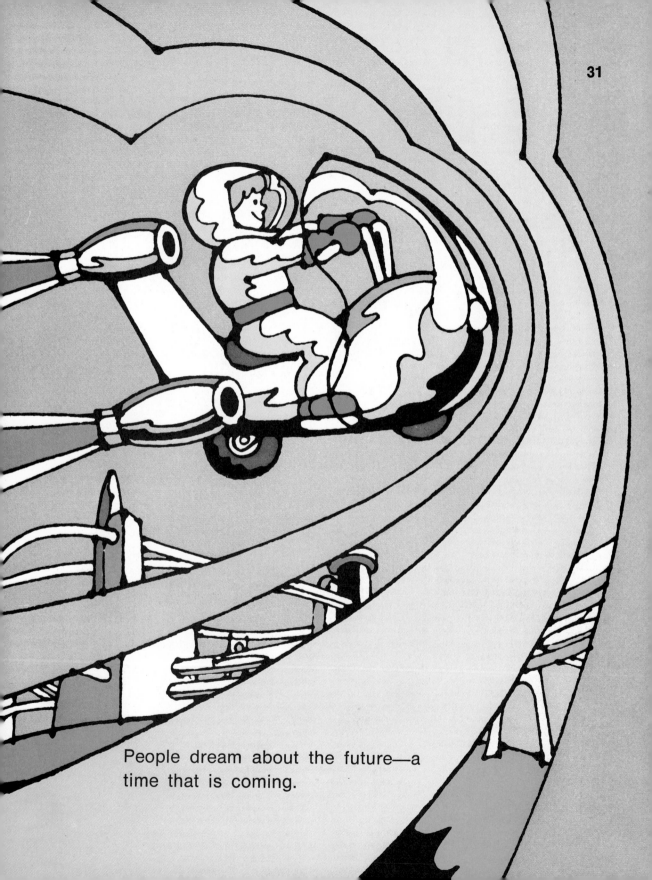

People dream about the future—a
time that is coming.

What is a person?
You will find out how people act by studying people using language, living in groups, using tools, and dreaming about things past and things still to come.

2

People Use Language

A gull says it is hungry by tapping the red spot on its mother's bill or on its father's bill.

A bird might tell it is hungry by its open beak.

When you were a baby this is how you told you were hungry.
You still use sounds to tell you are hungry. But now you use words.

Children from different places use different sounds to stand for milk.

Only people use written words to tell what they want.
This is a human thing to do.
This list will help a family plan for a future time when they will be hungry.

Words help us plan.
Words also tell us special things we need to know.
What kind of food is in this store?
How much food is in the box?
How would this help in planning for the family meals?

Writing may tell us what has
happened in the past.

I HAVE AN ANIMAL

WHAT SORT OF ANIMAL ?

I HAVE A CAT

WHAT SORT OF A CAT ?

⑤ I HAVE A GRAY AND WHITE PUSSYCAT

⑥ YOU'RE LUCKY YOU HAVE TWO PUSSYCATS

⑦ WHY DON'T PEOPLE UNDERSTAND ME?

Why is it hard to use words to tell what you mean?

PLAY

PLAY

A word can look the same, sound the
same but stand for different things.

When people speak they make sounds.

When people write they usually make marks on paper to stand for sounds they speak.

Picture writing is a special kind of writing.

It does not stand for sounds.

Pictures can tell a story without using words.

What story do these pictures tell?

One kind of picture writing can help
to answer the question.

Where on earth are you?

Long ago explorers went from place to place on earth, just as they do today.
They often went where no one had ever been before.
They made up a special language to tell other people where they had been.

The marks on a map tell many things.
Can you guess what some of these
marks mean?
To read marks like these, you need to
learn the language of maps.

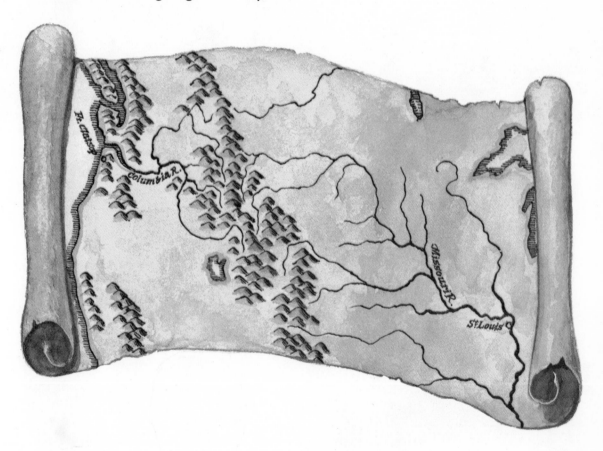

The marks on a map are called symbols.
Symbols stand for real things and places.
Which of these symbols tells about
the lake on this page?

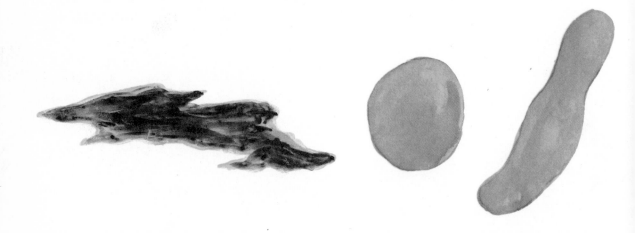

A symbol may say that a lake is
all alone in the middle of land.
A symbol may say that a river runs in one
end of the lake and out the other.
Can you find the symbol for a river?

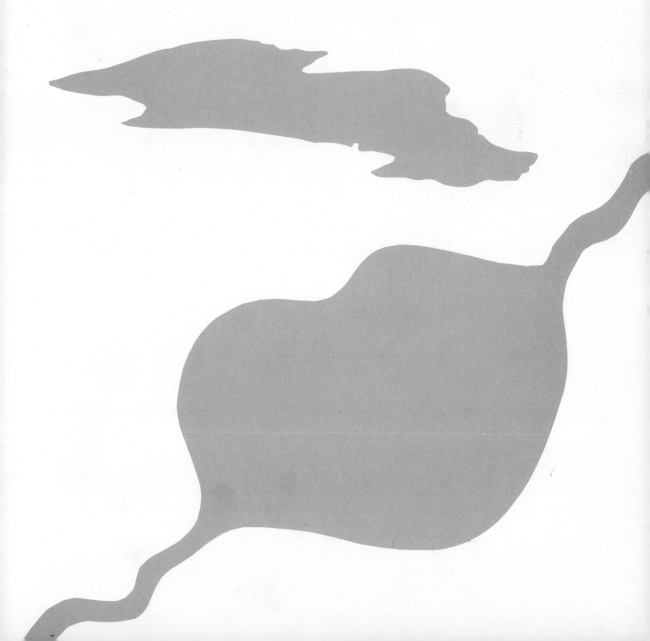

Map symbols can tell about what
someone sees on the earth.
What things do you see in the picture?
Here is how someone might make a map
to tell about the picture.

What does this symbol stand for?
Can you find it in the picture?
Can you find it on the map on page 52?

What does this symbol stand for?
Can you find it in the picture?
Can you find it on the map on page 52?

What does this symbol stand for?
Can you find it in the picture?
Can you find it on the map on page 52?

Cities are not all the same size.
Some are small.
Some are very big.

Can you guess which city on this page is
the biggest?
Which is the next biggest?
Which is the smallest?

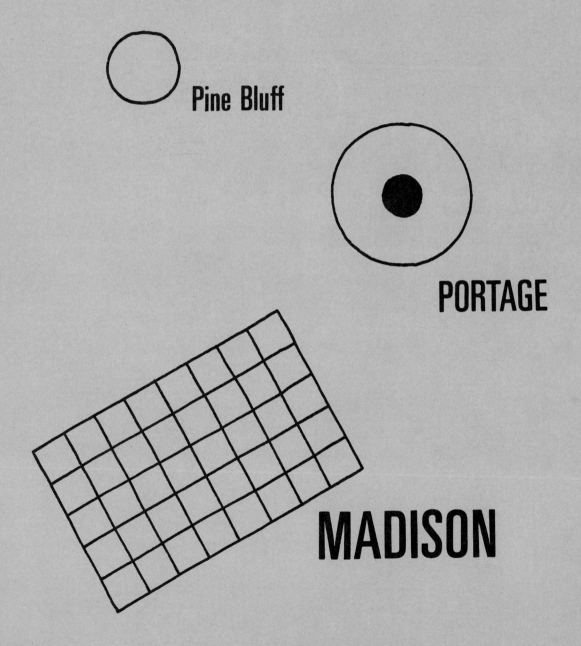

Pine Bluff

PORTAGE

MADISON

Can you tell why this symbol is used to show a railroad?

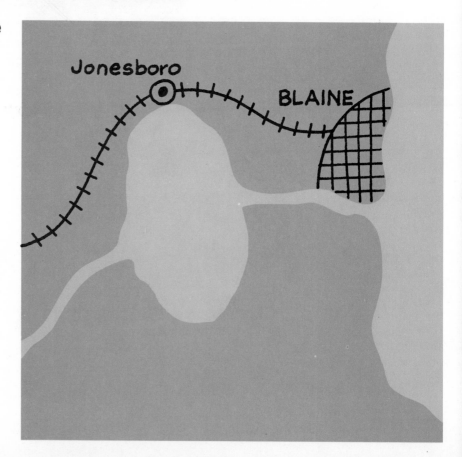

What do these map symbols tell you?

Jonesboro

BLAINE

Look at these words:
     street
     road
Does the word street tell you
where the street goes?
Does the word road tell you how
wide the road is?

The language of maps can tell you
how wide a road is,
where the road goes,
or if the road is straight or crooked.

What do you think the map language tells you on this page?

If you lived in this community, you might
use many words to tell a friend how to get
to your house from your school. It would
be easier to tell your friend if you used
the language of maps.

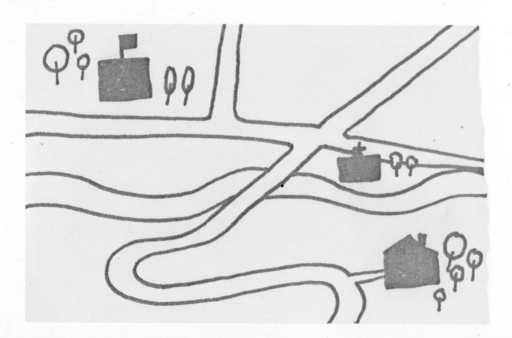

The language of maps tells about a place
on the earth.
What can you tell about this map?
Can you read your new map language?

Have people been everywhere?
The story of maps is an unfinished
story.
Maybe someday you will add
something to the story of maps!

3

What Is a Community?

This is not a community.

Tell what you can see in this town.
What is missing from this town?
Why is this not a community?

Does this community look like a
ghost town?
A community needs people.
To go on living a community must
have people.
Why does your family live in your
community?
What does it have that you need and
want?

Today many people live in or near a city.
What does a city have that people need?
One thing people need is water.
Most people want their water to taste good and to be clean.

People need a place to live.
Our world has many different kinds
of places.
People have learned to live in most
places by working together.

People can get the things they need
by working together.
Even if people have the same needs,
they may take care of their needs in
different ways.

How can Berbers meet their needs
in the desert?
Here water is scarce.
Water is hard to find.
People and animals need water to
live.

Berbers use animals for the
things they need. They get meat, milk,
and cheese from goats. Berbers
use camels to move goods from
place to place. They trade these
goods for other things they want.

One thing the Berbers trade
goods for is salt. They go to places
where salt is found. They trade
goods worth about 15 cents for each
large cone of salt. Then they go to
a place where they trade some of
the salt cones for cloth, leather, tea,
sugar, and knives worth about $1.50.

These Berbers live in a desert
community.
Where did they get the goods they
are using?
Why do they trade with others?

Here is another group of people
living in a desert community.
Name some things that these people
have.
How did they get these things?

The people in this
community earn money for the work
they do. They use the money to buy
things.

In a community people give
something for the things they get.
What is each person giving in these
pictures?
What is each person getting in
return?

In this community many people live very close together. Many cannot find jobs. Without jobs the people do not have the money to buy the things they need.

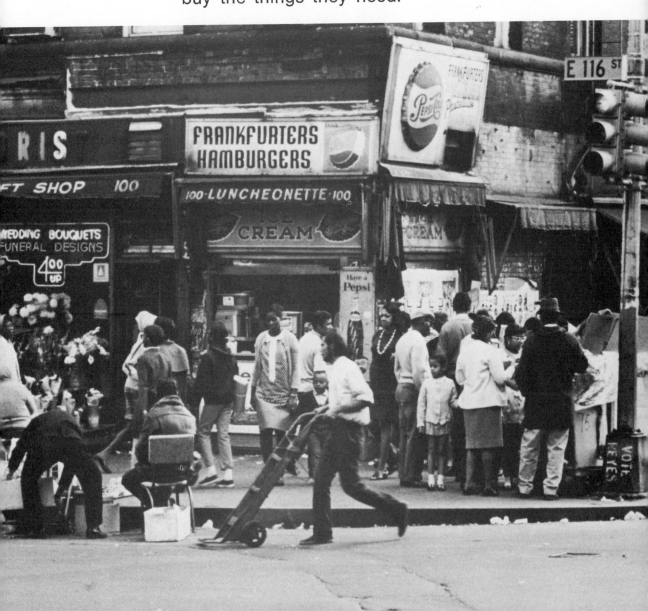

What is it like when people do not
have money to buy the things they
need?
People in this community dig coal out
of the mines in the ground.
How did digging coal out of the
ground change the land?

Today many of these mines
are closed. There are no jobs in the
mines. Will the people have money
to buy the things they need?

What things are made near where you live?

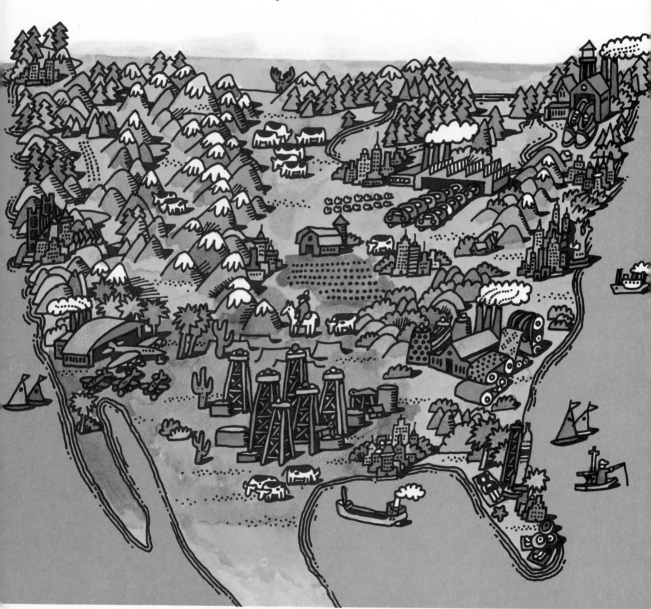

Name things that you get from far away.

People working together plan how
they will use the space they have.
Does your classroom look like any of
these places?
How could your class plan together
to use the space you have?

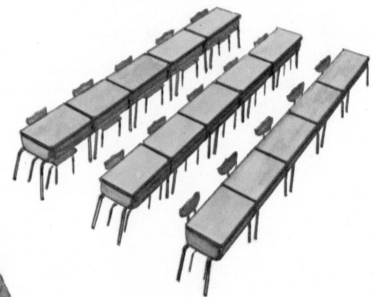

Communities plan to use space, too.

When people plan to use the same
space they need rules.
People have made the rules on these
signs.
How do these rules help you use
these places?

Rules help people work together. What are some of the rules these children might be following?

What rules are needed here?

When many people live in the same community, each person has less space to use. More rules are needed.

People are thinking of ways to get more space for living. Would fewer rules be needed?

Some houses might look
like this. Here glass is used to build
a house that looks like a bubble.
Would this give people more space?

People planning future cities think about how the land will be used. These cities could be built above or below the ground. They would not spread out over the land.

Some land between future cities would be used for growing food. This picture shows plans for future farms.

A greenhouse space ship may grow
the things you need.

Plans are being made to make city streets "people–places."

TV lets you see places that are far away. You can look but you cannot be there. What if you could walk around the TV set and see all sides of the things on the program. You would no longer have to go places. Places would come to you. Whatever happens, people are planning together to make the future happen.

4

People Use Tools

Without tools people are very weak.
They cannot protect themselves from
fierce animals.
They cannot hunt animals for food.

Your teeth are not strong enough to
cut down a tree.
They do not have to be that strong.

Long ago people learned to chip off bits of a stone. The stone became a sharp tool for cutting or chopping hard things.

Bushmen of Africa use tools
to help them hunt animals and get
the animals ready to eat.

These Bushmen are using
very old stone tools. A scientist
found the tools. He wants to see
if anyone can really use stone
tools to do hard work.

Long ago, no one knows when,
people learned that fire could also
be a very useful tool.
When people did not know how to
start a new fire they were careful to
keep some part of a fire always
burning.

Fire is a useful tool because it can
keep you warm when it is cold.
Fire can make food easier to eat.
Fire can keep away fierce animals.
Fire can even help make a boat.

Better tools help us do more work.
How have tools become better than
they were long ago?

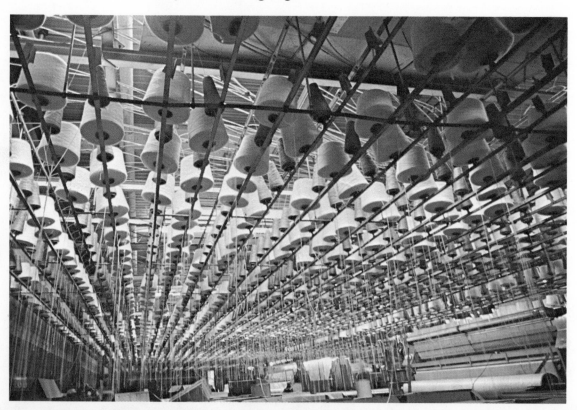

Some tools do more work than others because they use machine power, not just people power.

Farmers today can grow much
more food than farmers did long ago.
They use better tools for farming.

Some tools help people do work that would hurt them if there were no tools.

This tool carries metal that is so hot it has melted. It would burn anyone who touched it.

This tool handles things that are radioactive. Radioactive things would hurt anyone who touched them.

These people are using many
different tools to make a dress.

When people have jobs to do they
make tools that will help them.
Different jobs need different tools.

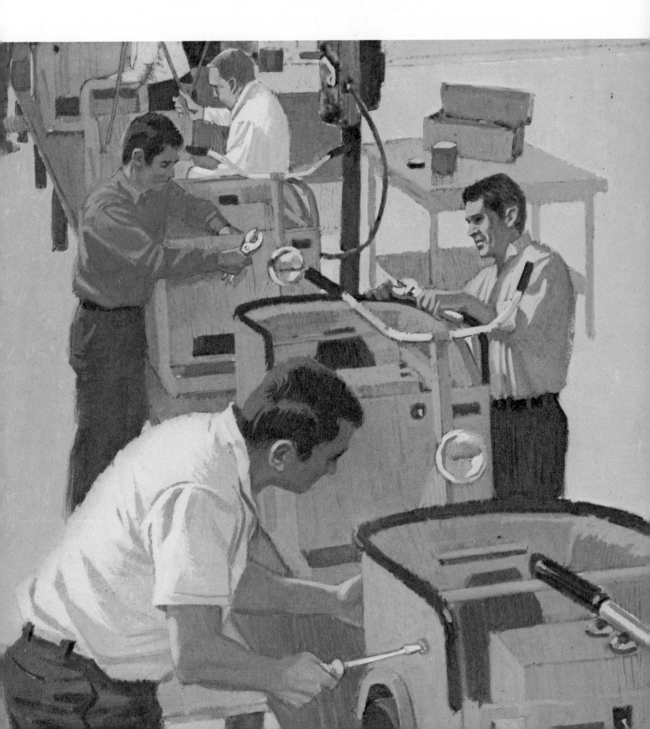

In her work this woman must write many letters. She talks into a machine.

Later her secretary will hear the words she said and will type them faster than she could write them by hand.

Mechanics do not make things to sell. People pay them to fix cars that were built by other people. Their tools are made for the jobs they do.

Artists need very special tools to
help them do their work.

Most paper is made in big factories. A factory makes enough paper in a day to fill a whole school with books.

Mr. Hamady makes paper all by himself. He makes his own paper to print a few books at a time.

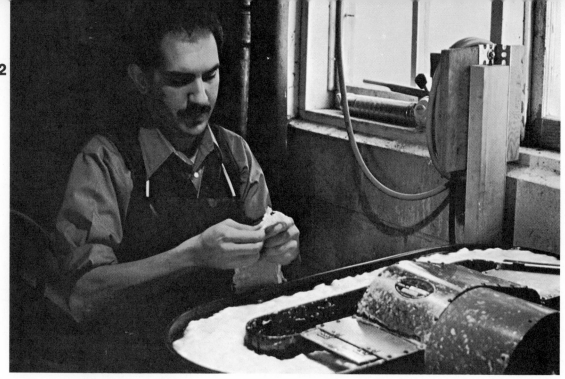

Mr. Hamady puts pieces of
rag in water. A machine beats the
wet rags into mush. A screen is
dipped into the thin mush. The mush
sticks together on top of the screen.

The screen is turned over
onto a soft pad. The mush has
become a wet piece of paper. A
machine squeezes the water out of
this wet paper. The wet paper is put
into an oven to make it dry.

The printing press prints two
pages at a time. The pages are put
together to make a book.

Miss Kreilick is an artist. She uses small stones to make pictures. Her stone pictures are called mosaics.

Miss Kreilick makes a drawing before she begins a mosaic.

Miss Kreilick uses big pieces of stone that have the colors she needs. Small pieces of stone are cut off the big pieces with a hammer.

The small pieces of colored stone are pushed into a sticky cement. When the cement is dry the mosaic is finished.

Mr. Latimer is an artist who
makes music. He makes music in
different ways.

What are some of the tools
Mr. Latimer uses?

Mr. Latimer plays in an orchestra.
He taps his drums softly to hear if
they are in tune.

He watches the orchestra leader
carefully so that he will know just
when to play his drums.

Many new tools are being made
today.
With these tools, people will do their
work better.

In the future, tools will do work for
people.
What tools will do work for you?

People Think About the Past and Future

When you were born you could not do very much. As time went by you learned to do many things. Can you remember learning how to ride a bicycle? Did you ever feel like this boy?

One of the ways some of us change is by learning how to do things. Can you swim? Can you play a piano? Can you drive a car?

Tell some other things you want to learn how to do in the days to come. People call the days to come the future.

Are you the same as you were when you were a baby? Of course not! No one is. As time passes, people get older and change in many ways.

Name some ways that these people are different from each other. Tell which people you think know how to read. Which ones know how to drive a car?

Which ones are the oldest? How can you tell? How do you think you will look in the future?

As time passes, people change. People change things, too. Long ago, in the past, people could not fly. They tried and tried to fly.

Ouch!

And they kept on trying.

Now look how people can fly!

Long ago people had to work very hard to get their food ready to eat. As time passed, people were able to change the way they got their food ready to eat.

What do you think schools looked
like long ago when your grandparents
were children?

As time passed, did people change
the way schools look?
What are some ways people have
changed how schools look since
your grandparents were children?

When your grandparents were children,
people rode from place to place in
cars.
Their cars were slow.
They made a lot of noise.
They often stopped running.
What cars!

When we think about the past, the things
our grandparents used may seem
strange to us.

Here is another look at the past.
This is what some things looked like
when your grandparents were children.

What things in the past do these
pictures show you?

Do these pictures look strange to
you?
These pictures were taken after you
were born.
That is not too long ago!

What do you think the pictures on
these two pages show?
What things have changed since
your grandparents were children?

As time passes, people are able to change most things to make them better.

Which cars are from the past?
Which car looks the most like a car of today?
Which car do you think is a car of the future?

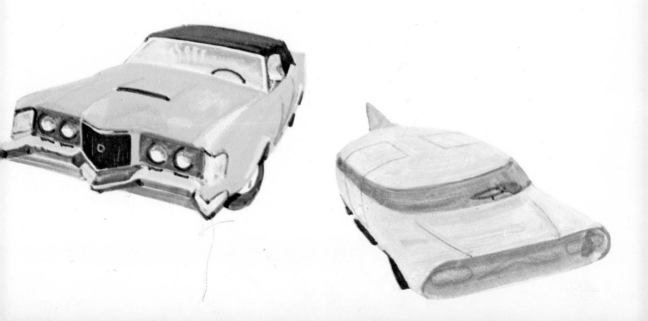

People have changed many things
about airplanes, too.

Which pictures do you think show
how airplanes look today?
Which pictures show how airplanes
looked in the past?
Which one shows how they might look in
the future?

What do you think is happening to
Tom's kite?

What happened first?
What things happened next?
What happened last?

When people make toys for you to
play with they start with a plan.

Before you can play with this toy,
it has to be put together.
There! This toy is finished.

Here is a picture story of someone's birthday party.
Something is wrong here.

Do the children eat the cake even
before they arrive?
Maybe you can tell this story the
way it happened.
What happened first?
What things happened next?
What happened last?

You have seen pictures from the past.

This is how some people think some
things will look in the future.
What do you think?

As time passes, people are able to change things and make them better.

By planning how things will look in the future, they are helping to make the future happen.

People just like you can plan to
make the future happen.
What did this girl and boy plan for?
How did they make the future happen?

You are an unfinished story.
What will your tomorrow be like?